CATS

MICHAELA MILLER

Contents

Words in bold, **like this**, are explained in the glossary on page 23.

Wild ones

Cats come in lots of different shapes and sizes. There are big wild cats like lions, tigers and panthers and small cats that we keep as pets.

lioness with her cubs

But whatever they look like, they are all related to wild cats which lived about twelve million years ago.

People first started keeping cats as pets about 4000 years ago. They were used to catch the rats and mice which ate people's food.

grey tabby cat

CAT FACT

Cats first came to Britain over 1000 years ago.

The cat for you

There are long-haired cats and short-haired cats.

Long-haired cats need help to keep their fur clean and tidy. They must be combed and then brushed every day to keep them healthy. This can take a long time.

Persian cats

CAT FACT

A fluffy kitten will probably turn into a long-haired cat!

Short-haired cats look after their own fur by licking it with their rough tongues.

5

Where to find your cat

Looking after a cat or a kitten is lots of fun. But it also takes lots of time and money. Before you get a cat, talk about it for a long time with your family. Make sure you can all look after a cat or kitten properly.

kittens in an animal shelter

There are lots of ways to find a cat or kitten. **Animal shelters** are often looking for good homes for cats. You could also ask a vet.

kittens

CAT FACT

Kittens need lots of attention. They also need to be toilet-trained.

A healthy cat - what to look for

The cat or kitten you choose should have a soft, smooth coat and clear, bright eyes. It should also have clean ears, a soft, clean nose and a clean bottom. A sneezing cat or one with a runny nose is probably not very well. Don't take it home with you.

CAT FACT

Some cats live for 20 years or even longer!

A healthy, happy cat or kitten enjoys playing.

9

Safe hands

Cats and kittens usually love to be stroked and held, but be gentle. Make friends slowly. Most cats like to be stroked softly around the ears and chest, and around their neck and back.

When you are allowed to pick up your cat, pick it up very carefully with both hands and support its bottom and hind legs.

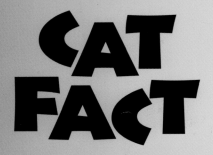

Holding on to a cat when it wants to get away will make it unhappy.

Feeding time

Cats need two or three small meals a day at regular times. Kittens need about three or four even smaller meals. Local shops and supermarkets sell cat food. Read the labels on the cat food carefully.

CAT FACT

Dog food should not be given to cats or kittens. It doesn't have all the right vitamins and minerals to keep them healthy.

You will need a bowl for food and a bowl for water. The bowls should be washed very well after each meal.

Home sweet home

Your cat will need a clean, quiet place like a basket or a box where it can sleep. It will also need a **litter tray** near by where it can go to the toilet.

The litter tray must be cleaned at least once a day. Even cats that like to be outside most of the time need litter trays. This is because cats need to be kept inside at night when most road accidents happen.

Cats can sleep between sixteen and eighteen hours a day.

Keeping clean

Cats are very clean. Your cat will spend a lot of time washing and **grooming**, so it won't need a regular bath. But it will probably like to be groomed gently by you with a soft brush.

mother cat grooming her kitten

CAT FACT

Cats can get worms which live in their stomachs and make them ill. Take your cat to the vet if it has worms.

You will need to check your cat for fleas. Fleas can live on the cat, bite it and make its skin itchy. If your cat has fleas, the vet can give you something to get rid of them.

At the vet's

Besides you, a vet is your cat's best friend. When you get your new cat take it to the vet for a check-up. Your vet will tell you when your cat should have **injections** to stop it catching **cat flu** and other horrible diseases.

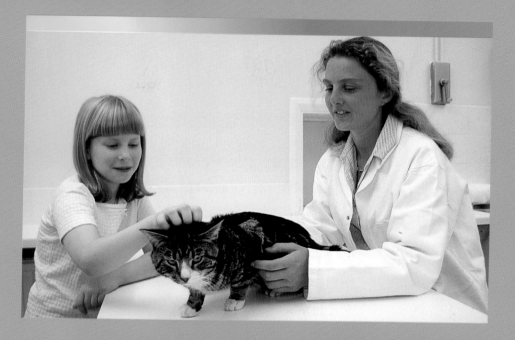

These injections are usually done once a year with a regular check-up and are very important. They could save your cat's life and also stop the disease spreading to other cats and kittens.

To find the name of a local vet, look under 'veterinary surgeon' in the Yellow Pages or ask friends who have pets.

No more kittens

There are lots of unwanted cats and kittens in the world and not enough people to take care of them. Don't let your cat – male or female – add to the problem. Your vet can tell you how **neutering** will help.

CAT FACT

A female cat which has not been neutered can have up to three litters of kittens a year, with five kittens in each litter.

mother feeding her young

Lots of owners find that their male cats are much easier to live with when they have been neutered. It stops them wandering off and fighting. Female cats will not have kittens if they have been neutered.

A note from the RSPCA

Pets are lots of fun and can end up being our best friends. These animal friends need very special treatment – plenty of kindness, a good home, the right food and lots of attention.

This book helps you to understand what your pet needs. It also shows you how you can play an important part in looking after your pet. But the adults in your family must be in overall charge of any family pet. This means that they should get advice from a vet and read about how to give your pet the best care.

Why not become a member of the RSPCA's Animal Action Club. You'll receive a membership card, badge, stickers and magazine. To find out how to join, write to RSPCA Animal Action Club, Causeway, Horsham, West Sussex RH12 1HG.

FURTHER READING

My Cat by Ruth Brown
Mrs Cockle's Cat by Philipa Pearce
Mog and Bunny by Judith Kerr

Glossary

animal shelters also known as centres or homes. There are lots of these shelters all around the country which look after unwanted pets and try to find them new homes. The RSPCA has about 50 animal centres in England and Wales.

cat flu a disease which can kill cats. They can be vaccinated against it.

grooming brushing and combing your cat

injections cats have to be vaccinated/injected by a vet to stop them catching diseases.

litter new born kittens

litter tray a box where a cat can go to the toilet. It has earth in it or special gravel called litter.

minerals like **vitamins** in food

neutering an operation to stop cats having kittens

vitamins all food contains vitamins. A good diet will have enough vitamins to keep humans and animals healthy.

Index

First published in Great Britain by Heinemann Library, Halley Court, Jordan Hill, Oxford OX2 8EJ, a division of Reed Educational and Professional Publishing Ltd

OXFORD FLORENCE PRAGUE MADRID ATHENS MELBOURNE AUCKLAND KUALA LUMPUR SINGAPORE TOKYO IBADAN NAIROBI KAMPALA

JOHANNESBURG GABORONE PORTSMOUTH NH CHICAGO MEXICO CITY SAO PAULO

© RSPCA 1997

The moral right of the proprietor has been asserted.

Designed by Nicki Wise and Lisa Nutt

Illustrations by Michael Strand

Colour reproduction by Colourpath, London

Printed in Hong Kong / China

01 00

10 9 8 7 6 5 4 3

ISBN 0 431 03364 1

British Library Cataloguing in Publication Data

Miller, Michaela

Cats. - (Pets)

1.Cats - Juvenile literature

I .Title II . Royal Society for the Prevention of Cruelty to Animals

636.9'3233

Acknowledgements

The Publishers would like to thank the following for permission to reproduce photographs.

Dave Bradford pp3, 5, 8-15, 17; Bruce Coleman Ltd/ p21 Jane Burton; RSPCA/ pp2 Julie Meech, 6 Colin Seddon, 4, 7 E A Janes, 16, 20 Angela Hampton, 18, 19 Tim Sambrook.

Cover photographs reproduced with permission of: RSPCA; Dave Bradford

Our thanks to Ann Head and her pets; Pippa Bush, Bill Swan and Jim Philips for their help in the preparation of this book; Pets Mart for the kind loan of equipment; the children of Oaklands Infants School.

Every effort has been made to contact copyright holders of any material reproduced in this book. Any omissions will be rectified in subsequent printings if notice is given to the Publisher.